ICELANDIC FOLK
AND FAIRY TALES

Retold by
Jón R. Hjálmarsson

25

ICELANDIC FOLK
AND FAIRY TALES

Translated by Anna Yates

FORLAGIÐ

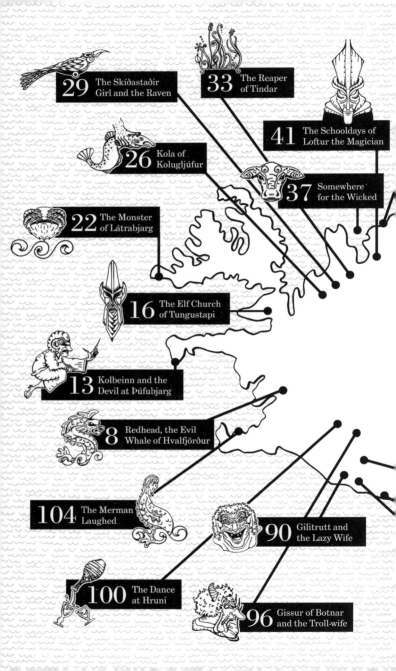

29 The Skíðastaðir Girl and the Raven

33 The Reaper of Tindar

41 The Schooldays of Loftur the Magician

26 Kola of Kolugljúfur

37 Somewhere for the Wicked

22 The Monster of Látrabjarg

16 The Elf Church of Tungustapi

13 Kolbeinn and the Devil at Þúfubjarg

8 Redhead, the Evil Whale of Hvalfjörður

104 The Merman Laughed

90 Gilitrutt and the Lazy Wife

100 The Dance at Hruni

96 Gissur of Botnar and the Troll-wife

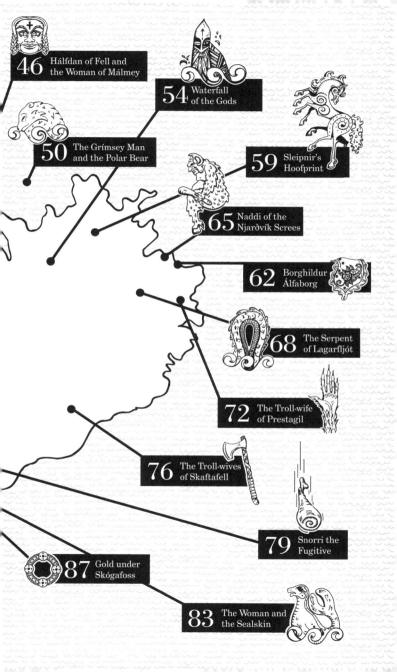

46 Hálfdan of Fell and the Woman of Málmey

54 Waterfall of the Gods

50 The Grímsey Man and the Polar Bear

59 Sleipnir's Hoofprint

65 Naddi of the Njarðvík Screes

62 Borghildur Álfaborg

68 The Serpent of Lagarfljót

72 The Troll-wife of Prestagil

76 The Troll-wives of Skaftafell

79 Snorri the Fugitive

87 Gold under Skógafoss

83 The Woman and the Sealskin

FOREWORD

Folk tales are an important part of any nation's cultural heritage. Iceland has a great and varied store of such tales, which give their own picture of the ideas and beliefs of past generations. Our tales tell of a wide variety of mysterious phenomena, including men with magical talents, "hidden people" or elves, ghosts, trolls, monsters, beasts and even the Devil himself, to name but a few. All the stories in this book are based on existing folk tales but have been slightly adapted and shortened, without altering the essentials of the tale.

I sincerely hope that readers will enjoy the tales in this book, whether they carry it with them on their travels around Iceland – or simply take an armchair tour through the nation's folklore.

Jón R. Hjálmarsson

REDHEAD, THE EVIL WHALE OF HVALFJÖRÐUR

Hvalfjörður is one of the more spectacular regions through which one passes on the way from Reykjavík to the north or west of Iceland on the Ring Road. Hvalfjörður (Whale Fjord) cuts into the land from Faxaflói bay, between Akranes and Kjalarnes. It is about 30 km long, 4–5 km across and 80 m deep at its deepest. In the outer reaches of the fjord there is some lowland, but towards the head of the fjord, steep cliffs rise straight from the sea. At its inland end, the fjord forks into two branches, Brynjudalsvogur and Botnsvogur. Hvalfjörður is surrounded by splendid mountains, such as Þyrill and Reynivallaháls in the south, and Múlafjall, Hvalfell (Whale Hill) and Botnssúlur at the head. To the east of Hvalfell is a large lake, Hvalvatn (Whale Lake), which is about 160 m deep. The river Botnsá flows from this lake and cascades down in the Glymur falls, by far Iceland's highest waterfall at 198 m. The origins of the place names Hvalfjörður, Hvalfell and Hvalvatn (Whale Fjord, Whale Hill and Whale Lake) are explained in an old folk tale:

Once upon a time some men from Suðurnes, on the Reykjanes peninsula, went out to Geirfuglasker (Great Auk Skerry) to catch great auks. When it was time to return to land, one of the men was missing. So the rest of the group returned home without him, and the man was believed to have died. A year later, however, the same men returned to the skerry and found the man, safe and sound. It transpired that elves had placed a spell on him and kept him with them, treating him well. But he was not happy with the elves, and went ashore with the other men. By now, however, an elf woman was carrying his child and she made him promise to have the child baptised if she brought it to him at church.

Some time later, the man was at mass at Hvalsnes church. A cradle was found outside the church, with a note which read: "The man who is father of this child will make sure that it is baptised." People were astonished, and the pastor suspected that the man who had spent a year on the skerry was probably the father. He pressed the man to acknowledge that he had fathered the child but the man denied it. At that moment a woman appeared, tall and robust. She turned to the man and said: "I cast a spell on you, that you shall become the worst of evil whales in the sea and wreck many ships." Then she seized the cradle and vanished without trace, but people assumed that she must have been the elf woman from Great Auk Skerry, where the man had stayed.

After this, the man went mad and took to his heels. He ran to the sea and jumped off the cliff named Hólmsberg, between Keflavík and Leira, where he was instantly transformed into the worst of evil whales; and he was called Redhead, for he had a red cap on his head when he flung himself into the sea. This whale proved a great scourge, and in the end he was said to have sunk nineteen ships between Seltjarnarnes and Akranes. Thus many people were harmed by him. As time passed, he began to take refuge in the fjord between Kjalarnes and Akranes, and so it came to be known as Hvalfjörður (Whale Fjord).

At that time, there was a pastor at Saurbær, on the shore of Hvalfjörður, who was both old and blind. He had two sons and one daughter, who were fully grown and very promising. This pastor had supernatural skills. His sons often went out fishing on the fjord. One day, they met with Redhead and he drowned them both. The pastor felt the loss of his sons deeply, and one day soon after this, he asked his daughter to take him down to the fjord, which was not far from the farm of Saurbær. He took a stick and made his way down to the shore with his daughter's help. Then he stuck his stick into the ground at the tideline and leant forward onto it. He asked his daughter what the sea looked like; she replied that it was mirror-smooth and calm. A little later, the pastor asked his daughter again what the sea looked like. Then the girl replied that she could see a black stripe coming up the fjord, like a big shoal of fish. When she told him that the stripe had reached them, the pastor asked her to lead him inland along the shore, and she did so. The stripe kept pace with them, to the head of the fjord.

But as the fjord grew shallower, the girl saw that the stripe was the wake of a huge whale, which was swimming straight up the fjord as if he were being led, or driven. At the end of the fjord, at the mouth of the Botnsá river, the pastor asked his daughter to lead him up the western bank of the river. She did so and the old man clambered up the mountain-side, while the whale struggled up the river next to them, with great difficulty, since the river was small and the whale big. When the whale reached the gully where the river cascades down off the heath, there was so little space for him that everything shook as he struggled on. Finally, as he climbed the waterfall, everything around trembled as in the greatest earth-quake and the rock made a thunderous roar. This is the origin of the waterfall's name, Glymur (Roaring), and the hills above the waterfall are known as Skjálf-andahæðir (Shaking Hills).

But the pastor went resolutely on, and did not stop until he had brought the whale to the lake from which the Botnsá river flows, which has been called Hvalvatn (Whale Lake) ever since. A hill that stands by the lake also derives its name, Hvalfell (Whale Hill), from this event. When Redhead reached the lake, he expired from the strain of climbing there. Nobody has seen him since, but impressive whale bones have been found at the lake and this is deemed to prove that the tale is true. When the pastor had brought the whale up to the lake, he made his way home with his daughter and everybody thanked him for what he had done.

KOLBEINN AND THE DEVIL AT ÞÚFUBJARG

Hellnar is a hamlet on the south coast of the Snæ-fellsnes peninsula. Here strange rock formations may be seen on the shore, including a cave known as Baðstofan (the baðstofa was the communal living/ sleeping room in a traditional turf farmhouse).

On the shore to the east are the Lóndrangar, rock pillars rising out of the sea, the tallest 75 m high. In times past, egg-gatherers used to climb the pillars in search of seabirds' eggs.

East of Lóndrangar is a small headland called Svalþúfa. Grass grows in the upper reaches, while a vertical cliff called Þúfubjarg rises from the shore, where the pounding of the waves has eroded caves and hollows in the cliff face. Bird life is abundant here, and the roaring of the sea mixes with the chat-tering of the birds. From here, it is just a short walk to Svalþúfa, which is a good spot for appreciating the natural wonders east of Malarrif – and for recount-ing the folktale of Kolbeinn, known as the "glacier-poet", and the Devil, who sat together on the cliff edge one night, exchanging verses, as the story goes:

nce upon a time, it is said that the Devil made a wager with Kolbeinn the glacier-poet. They were both to sit on Þúfubjarg cliff under the glacier, when the surf was at its wildest, and exchange verses. For the first part of the night, the Devil should compose the first two lines, and Kolbeinn should complete the verses, while during the second part of the night, the arrangement was to be reversed. And they resolved that he who could not complete a verse begun by the other should jump off the cliff and be from that day forth at the mercy of the other. And so they sat out on the cliff one night when the moon was shrouded in cloud. They exchanged verses all through the first half of the night: the Devil composed the first two lines and Kolbeinn completed the verses at once, with no delay. Then, in the second half of the night, Kolbeinn started composing the first two lines, and for a long time, the Devil was successful in completing the verses. When the night was growing old, Kolbeinn saw that this could not go on. He took a knife from his pocket, and held it up to the Devil's eyes, so that the edge seemed to touch the moon, and said:

Look upon this blade blade
let the moon oblige oblige

Now the Devil was speechless, for he could not find a word to rhyme with "oblige". He became quite uncomfortable and said: "That's not proper poetry, Kolbeinn." At which Kolbeinn completed the verse himself, saying:

you whom I have made made
fall when I replied replied you.

When the devil heard this, he was so taken aback that he fell off the cliff and down into the wave that broke below. It is unlikely that Kolbeinn had any more trouble with the Devil after this, and certainly he was never again challenged by him to exchange verses.

THE ELF CHURCH
OF TUNGUSTAPI

History and natural beauty combine with unusual power in the Dalir region of West Iceland. Sælingsdalur (Sælingur's Valley) is a verdant, picturesque valley which leads to the northwest from Hvammsfjörður and the Sælingsdalsá river meanders through. One of the estates in the valley, Sælingsdalstunga (tunga = a tongue of land), features in Laxdæla Saga: it was the home of Guðrún Ósvífursdóttir and her husband Bolli Þorleiksson. After Bolli slew his old friend and rival Kjartan Ólafsson, Guðrún exchanged homes with Snorri of Helgafell, who moved to Sælingsdalstunga. In Sælingsdalstunga, Snorri built a church of which one can still see some traces. Adjacent to the farm of Sælingsdalstunga, commonly called simply Tunga, is Tungustapi, an impressive rocky outcrop above the Sælingsá river. This has long been reputed to be the home of elves or "hidden people". It was said to be an elf cathedral and episcopal see. A folk tale says:

Many centuries ago a wealthy farmer lived at Sælingsdalstunga. His children included two sons, Arnór and Sveinn, both fine men, though in different ways. Arnór was gregarious and often amused himself with other youngsters. They would often meet up at the rock by the river known as Tungustapi. In the winter, they slid on the hard snow down off the rock, with shouting and merriment. Sveinn rarely took part in this; he generally went to church while the others were at play. He was also solitary and often went to the rock alone. It was the general opinion that he mixed with the elves; he disappeared on every New Year's Eve and no one knew where he went. Sveinn often asked his brother not to make so much noise by the rock, but Arnór mocked him and said he had no sympathy for the elves just because of a little noise.

One New Year's Eve, Sveinn vanished as usual. People started to wonder what had become of him and Arnór volunteered to go looking for him. He walked off in overcast weather to the rock. Suddenly, the rock opened up on the side that faced the farm, revealing innumerable lights within. He heard the most wonderful singing and he realised that the elves were celebrating Mass. Approaching, he looked through the door and saw the church filled with people. A priest in splendid vestments stood at the altar and there were many rows of lights on both sides. He walked into the church doorway and saw his brother, Sveinn, kneeling at the altar, while a priest laid a hand on his head. Arnór concluded that he was being ordained and called out loudly: "Sveinn, come, for your life is at stake." Sveinn was startled and made as if to go to his brother. At that moment, the man at the altar called out:

"Lock the church doors, and punish the human who has disturbed our peace. But you, Sveinn, must leave us, and that is your brother's doing. And because you placed more value on his call than on your ordination to the priesthood, you shall fall down dead the next time you see me here in these vestments." The men in their canonicals lifted Arnór, and Sveinn saw him vanish up into the stone vault over the church. At that moment, bells began to ring loudly and all those within rushed to the doors. Arnór ran home as fast as he could, hearing elves riding behind him with a clattering of hooves. He heard one of the leading riders chant:

Ride, ride, dark is the mountainside,
cavort, transport the wretch away,
never more to behold the light of day,
the light of tomorrow's day.

The riders swept by, between Arnór and the farm-house, and he had to retreat. On the slope below the farm, the elves rode over him and he was left lying more dead than alive.

Sveinn arrived home late at night. He was withdrawn and did not speak much, but he felt that a search must be made for Arnór. They searched for him all night, until finally the farmer of Laugar, on his way to matins, came across him on the slope, very weak. He told the farmer all that had happened that night, but he was too weak to be moved and he expired in that place, which has been known since then as Banabrekka (Death Slope). After these events, Sveinn was never the same again, growing ever more grave and melancholy. He soon abandoned all worldly things and became a monk at the Helgafell monastery. He was the most learned of men and sang Mass more beautifully than anyone else.

When Sveinn's father grew old, he fell gravely ill. And when he felt that he had only a short time left to live, he sent for Sveinn to come from Helgafell. Sveinn did as he was asked but said that he might not return alive. He arrived at Tunga on the Saturday before Easter, to find his father close to death. Sveinn's father asked him to celebrate Mass on Easter Sunday and gave orders that he should be carried into church, so that he might die there. Sveinn was reluctant but agreed, on condition that the church doors should not be opened during the Mass, as his life was at stake. This was regarded as a strange request but people concluded that he did not wish to see the rock: in those days the church stood on a low hill in the homefield and the church doors faced the rock.

The farmer was carried into the church and Sveinn donned his vestments and began to sing Mass. Those who were present said they had never heard such sweet singing or such excellent intoning, and they were as struck dumb. But when the pastor turned from the altar and began to pronounce the Blessing, suddenly a westerly gale struck, blowing open the church doors. The congregation were startled and turned to look. They saw what appeared to be an open doorway into the rock, from which shone innumerable lights. And when the congregation turned back towards the pastor, he had collapsed and expired. At the same moment, his father too had fallen from the pew and was also dead. The weather was calm both before and after this event, so it was clear to all that the storm from the rock was not a natural occurrence.

Among those who witnessed these events was the farmer of Laugar, he who had found Arnór at the point of death many years before, and he recounted the whole story. Then they understood that what the elf bishop had said to Sveinn – that he would fall down dead the next time he saw him – had come to pass. When the rock stood open and the church doors flew open, the doors faced each other, so Sveinn and the elf bishop saw each other – for the doors of elf churches face in the opposite direction to human ones. After this event, a regional meeting was held and a decision was made to move the church from the hillock down into a hollow closer to the farmhouse. This meant that the farmhouse stood between the rock and the church doors. Never again has the pastor been able to see through the church doorway to Álfastapi (Elf Rock) – and no such extraordinary events have happened since.

THE MONSTER OF LÁTRABJARG

*Látrabjarg (Látrar Cliffs), at the westernmost point
of the north coast of Breiðafjörður, are among Iceland's most impressive sea cliffs. The cliffs end at
Bjargtangar, the westernmost point of Iceland, and
indeed of Europe. North of Bjargtanger is Látravík,
and the farm of Hvallátur, the most westerly habita-
tion in Iceland.*

*Látrabjarg is 14 km long. All the cliffs are quite
high and most of them perpendicular. At their highest point, at Heiðnakinn, they rise 444 m above the
sea. Several small valleys cut into the cliffs. Many
of the gullies and rocky belts are rich in vegetation,
and in the past, they were even used for haymaking.
Many ships have sunk off Látrabjarg and many seamen's lives have been lost there. The last vessel to
run aground at Látrabjarg was the British trawler*

Dhoon, just before Christmas of 1947. All the trawler's crew members were rescued by local people, despite perilous conditions. But seamen were not the only ones at risk at Látrabjarg – those who climbed down the cliffs to collect eggs and trap birds were also in danger. The cliffs often yielded tens of thousands of birds in a summer and even more eggs, a valuable and prized resource. But traditional bird trapping and egg gathering on the cliffs has not been practised since 1925: the following year, two young men fell to their deaths, and after this, the custom ceased. There are many tales and traditions about Látrabjarg, including the following:

n the days of Bishop Guðmundur Arason the Good [13th century], it transpired that men were sure that a monster resided in Látrabjarg and was spoiling the fishermen's catch. Also, at that time, those who climbed down the cliff for birds and eggs had so many accidents that it was deemed suspicious. It often happened that when a climber was down on the cliff, those who were waiting above in charge of the rope suddenly saw that the man was gone – and later, he would be found, dead and mutilated, at the foot of the cliff. When the end of the rope was examined, it would appear to have been severed with a sharp blade. At that time, a man named Gottskálk lived at Hvallátur. He was a skilled man and was said to have mysterious powers, yet he had no effect upon this rock-dweller, although he is believed to have tried. Then Gottskálk and the others who used the resources of the cliffs took this problem to Bishop Guðmundur the Good. The bishop saw that action must be taken, so he went west to the cliff and summoned the rock-dweller to appear. The bishop upbraided him harshly for his persecution of the men, and said he would drive him off the cliff. The rock-dweller begged for mercy and asked to be allowed to stay, saying, "A black sheep must have somewhere to go." Then the bishop's ire was mollified and he asked the monster how much land he needed. The rock-dweller then said that the bishop could decide that himself, when he knew how big his family was. The bishop asked how many there were and the rock-dweller replied: "I have twelve ships off the shore; on each ship are twelve men, each man has twelve harpoons, and for each harpoon there are twelve seals. Then I cut each seal into twelve pieces, and there will be one piece for each of us and also two for each seal's head: so you count, sir."

And so the bishop gave the rock-dweller permission to live with his family in the part of the cliff that has since been called Heiðnabjarg (Heathens' Cliff). This was the part, stretching from Djúpidalur to Saxagjá, where it was most difficult for humans to trap birds and gather eggs. The bishop forbade the creature to go beyond these boundaries, and then he began to consecrate the cliffs. He consecrated all but Heathens' Cliff, and he forbade all Christian men to climb there or to utilise the cliff in any way. At this, the persecution by the rock-dweller ceased and he was never seen again – and the bishop's ban on gathering eggs and trapping birds on Heathens' Cliff was not broken for many centuries.

KOLA OF
KOLUGLJÚFUR

Víðidalur in northwestern part of Iceland is an attractive region, rich in history. At the old manor Víðidalstunga the Flateyjarbók (the Flatey Book), a large and beautifully illuminated book of saga manuscripts, was compiled in around 1400. Vellum prepared from 113 calfskins was required to make the book, which eventually made its way to the island of Flatey in Breiðafjörður, west Iceland – hence its name. Flateyjarbók was given to the Danish king in the 17th century but this national treasure was returned by the Danes to Iceland in 1971.

A short walk from the farm of Kolugil, the Víðidalsá river forms two spectacular cascades in a narrow gully, Kolugljúfur. The gully is about a kilometre in length and 40–50 m deep, with vertical rock walls in many places. Kolugljúfur is named after a gigantic troll-wife, Kola, who lived there once upon a time. This remarkable natural phenomenon can be seen from a bridge over the river to the west of Kolugil or from the edges of the gully on either side. This is the tale of the troll-wife Kola:

A short distance from the farm of Kolu-gil is a great gully, named Kola's Gully. In olden times, a huge woman named Kola is said to have lived there, and it is named after her. On the western side of the gully is a grassy hollow, still called Kolurúm (Kola's Bed), and this is where Kola is said to have lain at night when she wanted to sleep. At the front of the hollow are two thin rock pillars, which are called Bríkur (Bedposts). Between them is a gap, below which there is a cliff down to the Víði-dalsá river, which flows through the gully. When the giantess Kola wanted her breakfast, it is said that she reached down through the gap and into the river for salmon.

At the farm of Kolugil is a hill called Koluhóll (Kola's Hill). Underneath the hill Kola is supposed to have been laied to rest. Various attempts have been made through the years to dig up the hill but these have always been abandoned for one reason or another: once, the church at Víðidalstunga appeared to be on fire; another time, the river appeared to be flowing up the bank below Kol-ugil towards the farmhouse. Now there is a hollow in the hill, which is said to be two to three ells across [an ell is about 50 cm].

THE SKÍÐASTAÐIR GIRL AND THE RAVEN

At the mouth of the Vatnsdalur valley is a vast collection of hillocks, the famous Vatnsdalshólar (Vatnsdalur Hillocks), which are said to be innumerable, like the islands of Breiðafjörður or the lakes of Arnarvatnsheiði. The origins of the hillocks are not clear, but the commonly held view is that they were formed by a huge slide of rock from Mt. Vatnsdalsfjall in prehistoric times.

South of the hillocks is a large lake, Flóðið, which formed in 1720 when a landslide struck the farm of Bjarnastaðir, killing six people. The landslide dammed the river, forming a new lake.

Many landslides have fallen from the slopes of Mt. Vatnsdalsfjall to the east of the valley, leaving traces on the slopes and lowlands beneath. In addition to the Bjarnastaðir landslide mentioned above, an even larger landslide fell in 1545, laying waste to the farm of Skíðastaðir. Thirteen people died, but tradition says that one girl survived in an extraordinary manner:

ong ago at Skíðastaðir there lived a very wealthy farmer. He had many labourers on his farm and kept them hard at work both winter and summer. During the haymaking season he had the women servants cook meals only on Sundays, so that they could help with the haymaking on other days, and he would permit his workers neither to attend church nor to read the Good Book at home. Early one Sunday morning, a man dressed in white, and carrying a staff in his hand, was seen from many farms in the area as he walked northwards over Vatnsdalsfjall. He halted above Skíðastaðir and struck the mountain with his staff. Immediately a landslide began there, which grew larger and larger as it slipped down the slope. This awesome rockslide struck the farmhouse of Skíðastaðir, so that no living person survived except for one girl, who was at that moment away from the farmhouse.

This girl had been at Skíðastaðir for a long time, although she was not happy there and was dissatisfied with the farmer's godlessness. But she was kind and willing, and for this she was popular both with her masters and with the other workers. She often had to cook on holy days and received no extra reward, except that she was allowed to scrape the pot. The winter before the landslide fell was very harsh, so that both people and beasts died of starvation. The farmer of Skíðastaðir had plenty of everything but he refused to share it with others, though he was asked to do so, and he cruelly turned away all those who came in search of help. The girl, who cooked on Sundays, was sad not to be able to help the poor and hungry people, and she tried to give them some of her own food and the scrapings of the pots. The harsh winter was also difficult for all animals that had to be outside, so that they lay dead in piles. And crowds of ravens collected at farms to peck at any refuse that might be thrown out. The girl threw out as much as she could from the kitchen, for she was kind of heart and wanted to help the ravens, like the others. One of the ravens grew so fond of her that he followed her every step out of doors. In the spring and summer following that harsh winter, he arrived early every morning at Skíðastaðir, for the girl always kept some food for him.

On the Sunday morning of the landslide, the girl had risen very early to cook porridge. She hurried to finish scraping out the pot before the raven arrived, so that she could give him the scrapings. Just as she was finishing, she heard the raven croak outside. She took the scrapings outside in a ladle and placed them on the stones where she normally fed the bird. But the raven would not touch his food. He fluttered around and then flew a little distance out into the field. The girl followed with her ladle, but he did not want to eat there and flew farther off. So it continued: the girl followed the raven, trying to feed him, but he always flew up and went farther and farther away. The girl did not understand why the raven was behaving so strangely but she was determined to feed him. She followed him until he had led her some distance south of the homefield. The girl started to think that this was enough, that she must run back to the farmhouse. But at that moment she heard a roaring in the mountain, which preceded the landslide and the flood of water that accompanied it, and she saw this mass sweep over the farmhouse and right across the valley. And she thanked God with all her heart for sending the wise raven to save her.

THE REAPER
OF TINDAR

*The district generally known as Ásar stretches south
from Blönduós, the main town of Húnavatnssýsla,
between the river Blanda and Lake Húnavatn. It is
a rather low-lying area with few landmarks, through
which the river Laxá á Ásum (also known as Neðri
Laxá or Lower Salmon River) flows – one of the
most expensive salmon rivers in Iceland. The river
flows out of the Laxárvatn lake and into the sea at
Húnaós. The Fremri Laxá (Upper Salmon River),
on the other hand, flows out of Lake Svínavatn
and into Lake Laxárvatn, hence contributing to the
water-flow of the lower river. This valuable river was
harnessed at an early date to supply Blönduós and
nearby rural areas with electricity. The Ásar area
boasts many fine farms, as the soil makes for good
grassland. One of these farms is Tindar, which is
known for the following folk tale:*

nce upon a time there was a farmer at Tindar in Húnavatnssýsla named Árni Þorleifsson. He was an excellent farmer who also had some supernatural skills. One summer the grass in the fields was growing poorly due to cold weather and drift-ice close to the shore. Farmer Árni left his hayfields unmown during the summer in order to allow the grass to grow as much as possible. Others mowed their grass as usual, but even when they had finished their haymaking, Árni had not yet started to mow his grass. Shortly after this he asked the Devil to mow the grass on the homefield for him, in a single night. The Devil asked what his reward would be and the farmer said he might name his own fee. Then the Devil said he wanted the farmer himself in return. Árni agreed, on condition that the Devil mowed the whole field in a single night and finished before Árni rose in the morning.

The homefield at Tindar was very stony and in one place at the bottom of the field there was a rocky ruin known as Gníputótt. This was said to have been a chapel in former times and it was not possible to swing a scythe there without hitting a rock. Shortly after this, Árni prepared many scythes with sharpened blades. That evening he told the household to lie still and not move during the night. They did as he said, except for one old woman. She wanted to know what was going on, got out of bed and peeked out through the farmhouse door, which was open a crack. She saw a demon on every tussock and immediately went blind in the eye that had looked out; soon afterwards she went mad.

In the morning when the farmer came out, the Devil had mowed all the homefield except for the ruins mentioned before. He was struggling to cut the grass there and his scythe had grown blunt. When Árni went to him, the Devil was chanting this verse to himself:

At Gníputótt wherever I wield
the scythe-iron it strikes on stone.
Though Tindar is a slender field
it's tardy work for one.

He had mown all the grass but for two tussocks in Gníputótt. On one Árni had placed the Bible and on the other a book of Psalms, and the Devil eschewed such literature. Árni then said that the agreement was void, and told the Devil to go away and never come back. Gníputótt still bears the same name, and traces of it may be seen in the homefield at Tindar; below it is a marsh. It is clear that the wall around the homefield was formerly below the ruins, which were thus inside the homefield, as the story says.

SOMEWHERE FOR
THE WICKED

The island of Drangey is located on the western side of Skagafjörður, and is formed of perpendicular basalt, 180 m high. The rock can only be scaled at one point, known as Uppganga; the ascent is quite difficult, and at the top visitors must climb a metal ladder. At the top the island is about 0.2 km² in area, almost flat and very grassy. In the past, sheep were often pastured on the island, and the grass was also mown for hay. But Drangey is best known for its vast population of seabirds. Over the centuries, Skagafjörður people caught birds and gathered eggs in vast quantities: it is said that over 200,000 birds were sometimes caught there in a single spring, and the island was generally known as "Skagafjörður's pantry".

Drangey was never permanently inhabited but, according to the Saga of Grettir, in 1028–30 Grettir Ásmundarson and his brother Illugi survived on the island as outlaws until they were finally slain there. When the brothers' fire went out on the island, Grettir is said to have swum ashore to Reykir, a distance of nearly 7 km, to fetch embers.

here are many folk tales connected with Drangey. One tells of the origins of the island: two night trolls, who lived at Hegranes, were taking their cow to be serviced by a bull, for which they had to go all the way west to Strandir. They set off on their journey, the troll leading the cow, and the troll-wife walking behind. But they had only gone a short distance out into the fjord when dawn broke in the east and they were all turned to stone. The troll-wife is the rock pillar named Kerling (Old Woman) at the south of the island, and the male troll was another rock pillar, known as Karl (Old Man), which stood at the north of Drangey until it collapsed in an earthquake in 1755. The island, of course, is the troll cow.

Many lives have been lost on Drangey, as climbing the cliffs to catch birds and gather eggs was a hazardous pursuit. But long ago, people began to feel that there was something suspicious about the number of accidents on the cliffs, and it appeared that the climbing ropes had been severed by an axe or some other sharp weapon. These events were attributed to monsters or rock-dwellers who did not want humans from the mainland trespassing on their stocks of birds and eggs. This belief led to a decline in the utilisation of Drangey's resources.

In the early 13th century, Guðmundur Arason was Bishop of Hólar. He was a benefactor of the poor and other unfortunates, and was thus known as Gvendur the Good [Gvendur is a diminutive of Guðmundur]. He was renowned for blessing and consecrating many places in Iceland, including various wells, which are still known as Gvendarbrunnar (Gvendur's Wells).

The good bishop heard of the lives being lost on Drangey, which was in the possession of the episcopate of Hólar. He wanted to help, so he made his way to the island with his clergymen and holy water. On the way up on to the island he sang Mass at a rock shelf, which has been known since then as Gvendur's Altar. Everyone who visits Drangey says a prayer there. Now the bishop began to consecrate the bird cliffs with song, holy water and prayer. All went well until he arrived west of the northern end of the island. He was lowered on a rope there and began to bless the cliff, but he had not been speaking for long when a hairy grey paw emerged from the rock face, holding a sharp sword. The arm began to saw away at the rope where the bishop sat and two strands parted. But the bishop's life was saved because the third strand held fast – for it had been thoroughly consecrated. As this happened, a voice thundered from the rock: "No more blessing, Bishop Gvendur. Leave somewhere for the wicked." The bishop stopped his blessing and had himself pulled up to the cliff top. Thus a part of the cliffs was left unconsecrated. This place is called Heiðnaberg (Heathens' Cliff), and there are said to be more birds there than anywhere else on Drangey.

THE SCHOOLDAYS OF LOFTUR THE MAGICIAN

Hólar in Hjaltadalur, to the east of Skagafjörður, was for centuries one of the most important centres of power and culture in Iceland. Hólar stands in the middle of the Hjaltadalur valley, on a cluster of small hills formed by a slide of rock from Mt. Hólabyrða, the 1,244 m peak above Hólar. In 1106, the bishopric of North Iceland was established at Hólar; its first bishop, Jón Ögmundsson, later became an Icelandic saint. Bishop Jón founded a school at Hólar and paved the way for the establishment of Iceland's first monastery. Later bishops of Hólar included the renowned Guðmundur the Good, who is reputed to have consecrated wells, bird cliffs and dangerous paths all over Iceland. Jón Arason, the last Catholic bishop of Hólar, was executed in 1550 in the turmoil of the Reformation. Bishop Guðbrandur Þorláksson had an Icelandic translation of the Bible printed at Hólar in 1584.

Hólar Cathedral is one of Iceland's oldest stone buildings, consecrated in 1763, and many bishops of Hólar lie buried beneath the church floor.

Over the centuries, innumerable boys have sat in class at Hólar and gone on to serve as pastors. Most of them performed their duties admirably, although there were exceptions, like a certain Loftur, called "the Magician", who is well known in folklore:

oftur was a pupil at Hólar. He practised magic and urged his classmates to do the same, although they did little more than dabble. Loftur played many wicked tricks with his magic. One day he went home for the Christmas holiday: he took one of the maidservants of the place, fitted her with horseshoes and a bridle, and rode her home and back again by magic. After this, the girl lay ill for a long time from wounds and exhaustion, but she could tell no one of it while Loftur lived. He got another maidservant with child and killed her with spells.

Þorleifur Skaftason was pastor at Hólar Cathedral. He often upbraided Loftur, but to little effect. Loftur even played some tricks on the pastor, though without harming him, for the pastor had his own magical skills. Loftur learned all that was written in the Gráskinna (Greyskin) book of sorcery, but this was not enough for him. He wanted to gain access to the famous Rauðskinna (Redskin) book of sorcery, which belonged to Bishop Gottskálk the Cruel, who had taken it with him to the grave. Once, in early winter, Loftur spoke to one of his schoolmates, whom he knew to be brave, and asked him to help awaken some of the ancient bishops. This boy was to stand by the bell-rope and ring the bell when he received the signal. The lad agreed reluctantly, for Loftur threatened to kill him if he refused.

And so it was agreed, and on the chosen night they rose and went out into the church. The night was moonlit, so the interior of the church was fairly bright. The boy stood beneath the bells, while Loftur went to the pulpit and began to pronounce his incantations. Soon the ancient bishops rose from their graves, one after the other. They were dressed in white robes, with a cross on their breast and a staff in their hands. No sorcery was to be found among them, so Loftur redoubled his efforts, chanting the Psalms backwards in honour of the Devil. Then a thunderous noise was heard, and Gottskálk the Cruel himself rose up. He held a staff in his left hand and a red book in his right. He jeered: "You sing well, my son, but you shan't have my Redskin." Loftur chanted spells as never before, speaking both the Lord's Prayer and the Blessing backwards in honour of the Devil.

The whole church groaned and trembled. Gottskálk reluctantly held out to Loftur one corner of the book, and he reached out to take it. The boy took this for the signal he had been waiting for and rang the bell wildly. All vanished into the floor with a great noise, and Loftur was left alone, dazed and confused. Then he stumbled out to find his accomplice. After this, Loftur seemed to believe that he was doomed. He could never bear to be alone and he had to have a light when darkness fell. He was often heard to say: "On the fourth Sunday of Lent I shall be in Hell and torment."

Finally, it was resolved to send him to a god-fearing pastor at Staðarstaður, who had a reputation for curing the mad and victims of sorcery. Loftur improved considerably. The fourth Sunday of Lent came around, and the pastor was called out to minister to a dying neighbour. As soon as the pastor had left, Loftur rose from his bed and went to the next farm, where he persuaded a villainous old man to go out with him in a fishing boat. They went a short distance from the shore, in calm, fine weather, yet the boat was never seen or heard of again. Later, a certain man said that he had seen a hairy, grey hand reach up out of the sea, grab the prow of the boat, and drag both men and vessel down into the depths.

HÁLFDAN OF FELL AND THE WOMAN OF MÁLMEY

Málmey is a small island not far off the eastern shore of Skagafjörður. Low-lying at the southern end, the island grows higher to the north, and its highest point, Kaldbakur, rises 156 m above the sea. The island is green and fertile; it was inhabited for many centuries until 1950, when the farmhouse burned down and the last inhabitants moved away. Málmey has thus had a long and eventful history. Until the 18th century, the island had its own church, served by a pastor on the mainland. Various traditions were attached to Málmey; it was forbidden, for instance, to keep horses there, and if a couple lived on the island for more than 20 years, the wife would vanish.

Many renowned pastors served the parish in former times, some of them known for their supernatural skills. The most famous of these was the Rev. Hálfdan Narfason, who served the parish in the early 1500s. He was said to be a learned man, with great powers of sorcery. One of the best-known tales of the Rev. Hálfdan tells of the disappearance of the farmer's wife on Málmey, and of her husband's attempts to get her back with the help of the occult arts of the pastor at Fell:

n the days of Hálfdan, pastor at Fell, a man named Jón lived on Málmey island. He was a married man and wealthy, when this story begins. Jón had begun his farming on Málmey and lived there ever since. Now, however, the twenty years during which his wife was supposed to be safe on Málmey had passed, and nobody dared live there longer. But Jón, being a determined character and sceptical of superstition, decided to stay there, for Málmey was his inheritance. The twenty-first year now passed without event until Christmas. But on Christmas Eve, Jón's wife vanished and nobody knew what had become of her, though they searched far and wide.

Farmer Jón was most grieved by this and wanted to find out why his wife had vanished, so he went to see the Rev. Hálfdan at Fell and told him about his problems. The pastor told him that he could indeed find out what had happened to Jón's wife and where she was, but that would be of no use to her husband, as he could not get her back. The farmer asked if he could arrange for him to see his wife, as he felt it would be a comfort to him to know where she was. The pastor said he was most reluctant to do this, but when the farmer repeatedly begged him he agreed to do so. He told the farmer to come to him on a certain day, when everybody had gone to bed.

Farmer Jón arrived at Fell at the agreed time, and found the pastor awake and prepared to travel. A grey horse stood at the northern end of the church-yard, saddled and ready to ride. The pastor went to the horse and mounted. He invited Jón to sit behind him, saying: "But I warn you that you must not speak a single word, whatever happens. If you do, your life is forfeit." The pastor set off, and the farmer was astonished at how fast they travelled. They took the short-est route out to the mouth of the fjord, beyond Dalatá and Siglunes, and headed for Ólafsfjarðarmúli. Once the farmer was alarmed when the horse made a sud-den move, and he cried out. "It slipped on a skate: now shut up," said the pastor – and this has been a saying ever since.

No more is said of their journey until they came ashore north of Ólafsfjarðarmúli, where there were great, steep cliffs. They dismounted and the pastor went to the cliff-face. He took a little rod and knocked on the rock. After a short while, it opened and two women clad in blue came out, leading farmer Jón's wife between them. She was changed and quite unrec-ognisable – swollen and bluish, like a troll. The mark of the cross was visible on her forehead, in the true colour of her flesh. The Rev. Hálfdan later said this was the mark of her baptism, the only clue to her former existence. The woman spoke to her husband: "So you're here, Jón. What do you want of me?" The farmer was lost for words and the pastor asked him if he wanted his wife back, or to speak to her. The farmer said no. The pastor then gestured to the women to return to the rock and closed it behind them. He closed the doors in such a way that the women would pose no danger to anyone ever again. Since then, the place where the pastor opened the rock in the north of Ólafsfjarðarmúli has been known as Hálfdanarhurð (Hálfdan's Door). It is red and quite different from the surrounding rock.

The Rev. Hálfdan and the farmer of Málmey went back the way they had come and arrived at Fell before anybody was up. They dismounted in the same place by the northern end of the churchyard and the pastor removed Gráni's harness, accidentally slapping it on the horse's thigh. Gráni did not like this and kicked out at the pastor with his hind leg. The pastor avoided the blow, which landed on the churchyard wall, making a gap. It is said that however often the wall is repaired, the gap always opens up again. It is also said that no one has suffered any harm on Málmey since then, for no one has ever dared live there longer than twenty years.

THE GRÍMSEY MAN AND THE POLAR BEAR

Grímsey island is Iceland's northernmost community, intersected by the Arctic Circle. The climate of Grímsey is relatively mild and it has considerable vegetation. Many birds nest on the cliffs, where they are hunted and their eggs gathered for food.

Heimskringla, Snorri Sturluson's history of the Kings of Norway, tells how King Olaf Haraldsson coveted Iceland in the early 11th century. When his suggestion to take control of Iceland was rejected, it was proposed hat Iceland give Grímsey to the king as a token of friendship. Many thought this was a good idea, but Einar Þveræingur was of a different view: he pointed out that the king could maintain a whole army on Grímsey and attack the mainland at his pleasure. Convinced by his arguments, the Althing decided against giving the island to the king.

Polar bears have often drifted across from Greenland on sea ice and ambled ashore on Grímsey. One such bear was shot in 1969; it was stuffed and is on display at the Húsavík Natural History Museum. Folklore tells of another bear that visited the island long ago and received a rather warmer welcome:

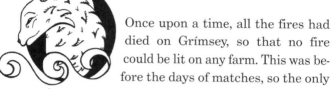Once upon a time, all the fires had died on Grímsey, so that no fire could be lit on any farm. This was before the days of matches, so the only option was to go to the mainland to fetch embers. At that time, the weather was very calm and the frost so severe that Grímsey Sound was frozen over. Three hearty men were sent ashore; they set off early in the morning in clear weather. Nothing is reported of their journey until they reached a gap in the ice. Two of the men jumped across, but the third was afraid. The two men went on, and told the third to return to the island. He did not like to turn back, and so he walked along by the gap, hoping to find a place to cross.

As the day went on, the sky grew overcast and a southerly wind came, bringing rain and wind. The ice then began to break up and finally the man found himself on an ice floe being carried out to sea. In the evening, he reached a tongue of ice and jumped on to it. But as soon as he had reached it, he saw a female polar bear with two cubs close by. The man was both cold and hungry, and now he feared for his life. The bear watched the man for a while, then stood up, walked over to him and gestured to him to lie down in her lair. The man did so, although he was apprehensive. Then the bear lay down and allowed the man to suckle her milk, like her cubs.

The night passed. The next morning, the bear stood up, walked a short distance from the lair and indicated to the man to follow. Then the bear crouched down and gestured to the man to climb on her back. He did so, and the beast then stood up. Then she shook herself so violently that the man fell off. Three days passed. The man slept in the bear's lair and drank her milk, and every day the bear had him climb on her back and shook him until he fell off. On the fourth morning, he did better and could cling on no matter how the beast shook him.

Later that day, the bear set off swimming with the man on her back and took him home to Grímsey. When they came ashore the man gestured to the beast to follow him. He took her to his home, had his best cow milked and gave her as much milk as she wanted, warm from the udder. Then he took the beast to his sheep-shed. He had his two finest sheep slaughtered, tied them together by the horns and hung them across the bear's back. Then the bear swam out to sea, to return to her cubs with the sheep.

The Grímsey folk now had reason to be happy, for as they were watching the bear's departure in amazement, they observed a ship approaching fast from the mainland. Their two messengers had arrived, bringing the much missed fire. Now all three men had returned, and the islanders could once again light fires and cook food.

WATERFALL OF THE GODS

Iceland boasts a multitude of waterfalls of all shapes and sizes. Wide and narrow, high and low, large and small, famous and obscure, their variety is almost inexhaustible. One of the most picturesque and famous waterfalls in Iceland is Goðafoss (Waterfall of the Gods), in the Skjálfandafljót river; most travellers in the north stop to admire it.

Nearby, in Ljósavatnsskarð pass, lies the delightful Ljósavatn lake. To the left is Kaldakinn, while ahead and to the right is Bárðardalur. Through this valley flows the powerful Skjálfandi river, and straight ahead, the spray can be seen rising from Goðafoss.

Just south of Ljósavatn lake is a very old farm of the same name. Around the year 1000, this was the home of Þorgeir Þorkelsson, chieftain of Ljósavatn, who played a crucial role in Icelandic history. It is to him that Goðafoss owes its name.

Although our tales of Goðafoss are drawn not from folklore but from saga literature, they nevertheless have a strong flavour of folk tradition:

orgeir was the Law Speaker at the Althing who made the fateful decision in AD 1000 that Iceland should become a Christian nation. He himself believed in the old Norse gods when he rode to the Althing that summer, but after the assembly had agreed to his proposal that all Icelanders should be baptised as Christians, he was probably among the first to receive baptism. And so he returned to his home a Christian and had to change all his customs. He set an example by removing all the idols of the Norse gods from his temple, taking them to the Skjálfandi river and flinging them into the water at a great waterfall, which was named after this event and has been known ever since as Goðafoss (Waterfall of the Gods).

The Saga of Grettir also tells a story of a waterfall; although the waterfall is not named in the story, it appears to be Goðafoss.

The outlaw Grettir Ásmundarson was hiding out at the farm of Sandhaugar in Bárðardalur. It so happened that during the past two Christmases, the men who were left behind to guard the farm while the rest of the household went to Mass had vanished. First it was the farmer himself, Þorsteinn, who vanished, and the next year, a farmhand. Grettir offered to stay home alone and guard the farm on Christmas night. After the people of the household had left, he prepared himself as well as possible, and at first all was quiet. But in the middle of the night he heard a commotion and in came a fearsome troll-wife. She attacked Grettir and they wrestled for a long time, first indoors, then out of doors and far and wide. The troll-wife did her best to haul Grettir down to the river canyon and throw him over the cliffs. She almost succeeded but then Grettir managed to free his right hand and grab his axe. He chopped at her arm, so that it came off and the troll fell into the canyon and the waterfall there.

Grettir was exhausted after this struggle but soon recovered, thanks to the good care of Steinvör, the woman of the house at Sandhaugar.

Grettir suspected that there were more trolls in the river canyon. Soon after Christmas, he asked Father Steinn of Eyjadalsá to explore the waterfall and its surroundings with him. They thought they could see caves behind the waterfall and Grettir wanted to examine them better, although they were difficult to reach. He took the priest along to look after the rope. After that, he prepared for his expedition: he wore few clothes and put his axe in his belt, bearing no other weapon. Then he jumped off the cliff and into the waterfall. The priest saw the soles of his feet, but did not see what became of him. Grettir dived beneath the waterfall, which was difficult due to eddies, and he had to dive down to the bottom before he could come up under the waterfall. There was a rock there, so he could climb up. He saw a huge cave where the river cascaded over the falls. He entered the cave and saw a great fire and a fearsome giant sitting there. When Grettir reached him, the giant jumped to his feet, grabbed a big spear and struck out at him. Grettir struck back with the axe, hitting the spear shaft so that it fell into two pieces. The giant then reached for a sword that hung in the cave. Grettir struck at the giant's breast, so that almost all his chest and belly were cut off and all his guts tumbled into the river. As the priest sat by the rope, he saw the bloody guts carried along by the current. Then he left the rope and ran all the way home. Evening had come and the priest said that Grettir was certainly dead by now.

But Grettir did not give up until the giant was dead. Then he lit a light and went farther into the cave to explore. It is not known how much treasure he found but it is said to have been considerable. He remained there for much of the night. He found the bones of two men and took them with him in a sack. Then he left the cave and returned to the rope and shook it, for he thought the priest was there to pull him up. When he realised the priest had gone, he had to climb up by his own strength and he reached the cliff. Then he went to Eyjadalsá and left the sack of bones he had found in the cave in the vestibule of the church, so that they might later be buried in hallowed ground. After Grettir's feat, trolls and other monsters caused no more harm in Bárðardalur.

ÁSBYRGI: SLEIPNIR'S HOOFPRINT

Ásbyrgi (the Gods' Bastion) is a huge depression in the earth, 3.5 km long and more than one kilometre across, surrounded by near-vertical cliffs 90–100 m high. The entrance opens up like a portal to a fairy-tale castle and is divided in two by a tall rock named Eyjan (The Island). The bottom of Ásbyrgi is almost flat, with abundant vegetation and birch woods. And in the south of this natural fortress lies a small lake, Botnstjörn.

The origin and formation of Ásbyrgi have long been disputed by geologists, but the consensus now seems to be that Ásbyrgi was formed in massive floods of the Jökulsá river at the end of the last Ice Age, 8–10,000 years ago, and then again about 3,000 years ago. Following this, the river is believed to have cut itself a new course, flowing into its canyon by the farm of Austaraland. Of the many waterfalls in the river, Dettifoss is the largest, 44 m high and the most powerful waterfall in Europe. The Jökulsárgljúfur canyon and its surroundings have been a National Park since 1973.

While scientists claim that Ásbyrgi and Jökulsár-gljúfur were formed in a huge flood, there are other theories as to how these formations originated. All these events took place thousands of years before man set foot in Iceland, so no witnesses can be produced to verify them. But there is an old folk tale:

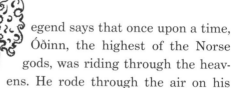

egend says that once upon a time, Óðinn, the highest of the Norse gods, was riding through the heavens. He rode through the air on his eight-legged stallion Sleipnir, among the Northern Lights in a starlit sky. The god was a little careless with the reins, riding high and low, not always looking where he was going, and one time he came a little too close to the earth, so that Sleipnir touched the ground with one of his eight hooves, treading down hard. This tore the surface and the earth collapsed underneath. The hoof-print left by Sleipnir is clearly visible today, and is called Ásbyrgi (the Gods' Bastion).

This old tale may well be deemed as good an explanation of the origins of Ásbyrgi as any other. Certainly, all who visit this place will be touched by its beauty and splendour; the thought may even occur that this magnificent cliff-lined fortress must surely be the work of the gods.

BORGHILDUR OF ÁLFABORG

Borgarfjörður is one of the most picturesque places in Iceland and it is also famed for its rich heritage of folklore. Between Njarðvík and Loðmundarfjörður, it is the northernmost of the fjords that cut into the highlands of the East Fjords. In recent times, a village named Bakkagerði has grown up at the head of the fjord. In the lowlands at the village of Bakkagerði stands a rocky hill known as Borg or Álfaborg (Elf Rock). This attractive feature has long been believed to be one of the main centres of Iceland's elf population. Over the years many people have seen these graceful beings.

The church, which is close to Álfaborg, contains an interesting altarpiece painted by Jóhannes Sveinsson Kjarval (1885–1972), one of Iceland's leading 20th century artists. The altarpiece depicts the Sermon on the Mount; Christ stands upon Álfaborg, with the Dyrfjöll mountains in the background. The altarpiece was controversial when painted, as some deemed it too "worldly" for a church.

The Borgarfjörður tales of elves or "hidden folk" are unusually imaginative. For example:

nce upon a time a farmer lived at Jökulsá, which is the closest farm to Álfaborg west of the Fjarðará river. He had a maidservant whose name was Guðrún. One Sunday in summer, the entire household went to church at Desjarmýri, except the maidservant Guðrún. Her mistress asked her to round up the sheep and milk the ewes. Then she was to skim the milk and churn the butter. The household went off to church and the girl set off to round up the sheep. When she had milked the ewes, she let them out on to the gravel banks below the farm. Then she started to cook dinner and when she had finished her work, she went outside to look out for the ewes and take a look around. She saw many people riding along the path below the homefield. They were wearing brightly coloured clothing and rode fine, spirited horses. She was most astonished, for everybody should have left for church earlier. All these people rode by the farm, except for one woman, who rode up the homefield to the farmhouse.

The woman was quite elderly, but looked well and had a noble countenance. She greeted the girl and said: "Give me some buttermilk to drink, my girl." Guðrún ran indoors, filled a wooden jug with buttermilk and brought it out to her, and the woman took the jug and drank. When she looked up from the jug, the girl asked: "What is your name?" The woman did not reply, but drank again. The maidservant then asked the same question again. When the woman had drunk from the jug and replaced the lid, the girl saw that she reached into her bodice, took a beautiful linen cloth, placed it over the jug lid and passed it to her as she thanked her. Then the girl asked a third time: "What is your name?" "My name is Borghildur, Miss Curiosity," said the woman as she spurred her horse and rode away from the farm to follow the rest. Guðrún the maidservant watched them; the last thing she saw was that they disappeared behind a grey rock at Kollutungur, which leads to Kækjudalur.

After a long time, the people of the household returned from church in the evening. The girl then told them what had happened during the day and showed them the cloth the woman had given her. It was so beautiful that nobody had ever seen such a fine cloth. It is said to have been passed down among Icelandic gentlewomen through the ages. The riders seen by the maidservant were believed to have been elves from Álfaborg, on their way to church in Kækjudalur.

NADDI OF THE NJARÐVÍK SCREES

Njarðvík is the northernmost bay of the East Fjords. Traces of an old wall, Þorragarður, which is believed to have been built by the Saga-age chieftain Ketill Þrymur, may be seen there.

From Njarðvík, the road leads on towards Borgar-fjörður eystri, following a steep mountain slope known as Njarðvíkurskriður (Njarðvík Screes), a fearsome place to travel in former times. It was not uncommon for people to lose their lives along the way, not least in avalanches. The most recent deaths were in 1909, when two men perished there.

In the past, the deaths on the Njarðvík Screes were attributed to a creature known as Naddi, reputed to live in a cave in Naddagil (Naddi's Gully), to the north of the screes. Naddi was eventually defeated and after this, a wooden cross was raised on the road, bearing a Latin inscription. The cross has been renewed many times and it remains in place today. The inscription reads in translation: Bow down and revere / this effigy of Christ, / you who pass by. / AD 1306.

Naddi was said to be a monstrous creature, with the upper body of a man and the lower body of a beast. He was rarely seen during the light months of summer, but often attacked travellers when the nights began to draw in, and killed many of them.

An old tale tells of Naddi's demise:

One day in late autumn, Jón Bjarnason was on his way home to Njarðvík from Borgarfjörður. Along the way he called at Snotrunes, arriving there at sunset. The people there asked him to spend the night and not to risk the Screes so late in the evening. He said that nothing would happen to him and he continued his journey, but when he reached Naddagil, the creature attacked him. There was a great struggle between them, which lasted a long time. They went far and wide in their fighting and eventually came to Krossjaðar, where the creature escaped from Jón and slipped down into the sea. A cross was later erected on that spot, with a Latin inscription saying that travellers should bow down and pray there. After the confrontation with Naddi, Jón reached home at Njarðvík. He was in pain, black and blue with bruises, and he lay in his bed for a month before he was able to get up. But the creature was never seen again after their struggle. Jón believed that it must have come from the sea, since it returned there after being defeated in the fight.

THE SERPENT OF LAGARFLJÓT

The Lagarfljót river forms Iceland's third-largest lake, about 52 km2 in area, 35 km long and from 1 to 2.5 km across. The lake's most notable statistic, however, is its depth, which is up to 112 m. The surface of the lake lies 22 m above sea level, so at its deepest, the lake floor is 90 m below sea level. The lake is always coloured a murky brown by glacial sediment, and in several places natural gases bubble up from the bed, so it rarely freezes in winter. This has lent it an air of mystery, and folk tales have been told of it since time immemorial.

According to folklore, a monster lives in the depths of the Lagarfljót. The Lagarfljót Serpent is reputed to have been seen by many people over the centuries.

One or more loops of the serpent's body were said to be glimpsed rising out of the water and this was regarded as an evil omen. The serpent never caused any real harm, however, as he was said to have been fettered to the bottom of the lake long ago. In modern times, belief in the serpent has waned, and some maintain that the "monster" was nothing but flotsam and jetsam on the surface of the lake. Yet there are always those who reject such rationalist explanations, and choose to believe that there really is a serpent; after all, the lake is so large and so deep that it may conceal mysteries of which we know nothing. One folk tale of the serpent says:

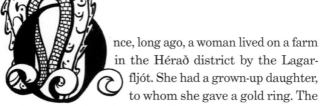

nce, long ago, a woman lived on a farm in the Hérað district by the Lagar- fljót. She had a grown-up daughter, to whom she gave a gold ring. The daughter asked her how she could derive the great- est benefit from the gold, and her mother told her to place the ring beneath a heather-serpent. The girl took a heather-serpent, placed the gold ring beneath it and put them both in her linen chest. The serpent lay there for several days. But when the girl went to check on the chest, the serpent had grown so big that the chest was bursting apart. The girl was frightened, so she took the chest and threw it into the river, serpent and all.

Some time later, people began to see the serpent in the lake, and it started to kill both men and beasts there. Sometimes, it also stretched up on to the banks and spewed a horrible poison. People were very con- cerned about this, but they did not know how to deal with the problem. Finally, two skilled Finns were brought to Iceland. They were commissioned to kill the serpent and fetch the gold.

The Finns jumped into the river, but soon returned to the surface. They said the case was hopeless, for the serpent was unbeatable; it was neither possible to kill the serpent nor to get the gold. They also said that another serpent lay under the gold, far fiercer than the first. But they dived down again and again, and finally managed to fetter the serpent in two places: one fetter was behind the flippers, the other in front of the tail. Since then, the serpent has been able to kill neither man nor beast, but sometimes it flexes its back up out of the water. When this is seen, it is generally deemed a bad omen.

THE TROLL-WIFE
OF PRESTAGIL

*Mjóifjörður, one of the numerous East Fjords, cuts
into the mainland between Norðfjörður and Seyðis-
fjörður. It is about 18 km long and about 2 km across
in its outer reaches, though narrower farther inland.
There is little lowland in the fjord, which is enclosed
on both sides by high mountains; the fjord is so narrow that on some farms, the sun is not seen for many
months during the winter.*

*At the head of the fjord once stood the manor of
Fjörður, which was inhabited into the 20th century;
for hundreds of years, it had a church and resident
pastor, and the churchyard, of the old circular type,
may still be seen to the east of the farmhouse site.
In the late 18th century, Fjörður ceased to have a
resident pastor, but the church remained there until
1891, when it was moved down to Brekka, a hamlet
that stands farther out by the fjord.*

*A lighthouse stands at Dalatangi, the outermost
point on the northern shore of Mjóifjörður. In former
times, there were several farms at Dalakálki, inland
from Dalatangi, but these have now all been abandoned, like most others in the fjord. The landscape
here offers strange and beautiful rock formations,
which have no doubt given rise to folk tales such as
this one:*

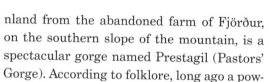 nland from the abandoned farm of Fjörður, on the southern slope of the mountain, is a spectacular gorge named Prestagil (Pastors' Gorge). According to folklore, long ago a powerful troll-wife lived there, who used her magical powers to enchant the pastors of Fjörður, so that she could devour them. She would go to the church when the pastor was in the pulpit and wave her hand rhythmically outside the pulpit window, until the pastor went mad and cried out:

> *Tear out my guts and my heart,*
> *off to the gorge I'll depart.*
> *Tear out my lust and my seed,*
> *to Mjóifjörður gorge I shall speed.*

After this, he would run out of the church, into the gorge, and never be seen again.

One day, a traveller passed by the gorge. He saw a troll-wife sitting on the cliff top, holding something in her hand. The man asked her what it was and she said she was nibbling at the Rev. Snjóki's skull. The traveller told of what he had seen and this was regarded as bad news.

So it continued for a long time; the pastors of Fjörður vanished, one after the other. This became a problem, for clergymen grew reluctant to serve the parish. Finally, no pastor could be found. Then one clergyman volunteered to go to Fjörður, despite knowing of the creature in the gorge. Before he celebrated Mass there for the first time, he gave instructions as to what should be done if he behaved strangely in the pulpit. Six men were to hurry to hold him still, another six were to go to the church bells and ring them, and ten were to go to the church doors. When this had been decided, the pastor began to say Mass. All went well until he stepped into the pulpit. Then a hand appeared at the pulpit window, waving wildly outside. The pastor went mad and began to chant:

Tear out my guts and my heart,
off to the gorge I'll depart.
Tear out my lust and my seed,
to Mjóifjörður gorge I shall speed.

He made as if to rush out of the church, but then the six men seized him, the other six rang the church bells energetically and ten hurried to the doors. When the troll-wife heard the bells, she ran off. She jumped on the churchyard wall, making a large gap. Then she said: "You shall never stand," and since then, the gap in the wall has always opened up again, however well it is repaired. But the troll-wife ran in a panic into the gorge and was never seen again.

The troll-wife is said to have lost the iron shoe off one of her feet when she kicked at the churchyard wall. Hermann Jónsson of Fjörður, who died in 1837, said he remembered this iron shoe, which was used for refuse.

A rock at Prestagil is called Skrúði (Vestments) or Skrúðasteinn (Vestment Rock). The doomed pastors are supposed to have placed their vestments here before they rushed into the gorge to the troll-wife. A rock in the gully is known as Líksöngshamar (Requiem Rock); this is said to be where the pastors howled and screamed as the troll-wife tore them to pieces.

THE TROLL-WIVES OF SKAFTAFELL

Skaftafell lies at the roots of Vatnajökull and has been a national park since 1966. Among many other natural attractions is the beautiful waterfall Svartifoss (Black Falls), where the river cascades over a natural "vault" of columnar basalt.

Tradition says that long ago, the glaciers were much smaller than they are today, and that there was once a route that passed across the highlands through the middle of the Vatnajökull glacier. The farmer of Möðrudalur, north of the glacier, 170 km away as the crow flies but twice as far by road nowadays, is said to have had rights to cut trees at Skaftafell, while the farmer at Skaftafell had the right to graze horses at Möðrudalur. The shepherd at Möðrudalur was supposed to have his own bed at Skaftafell, and the Skaftafell shepherd at Möðrudalur, indicating that there was once frequent contact between the two farms.

Many renowned men have lived at Skaftafell. The skill and knowledge of such men often gives rise to folk tales, suggesting that their skills were not entirely of this world; some of the Skaftafell farmers were supposed to be familiar with the troll-wives of the Skaftafell mountains:

Long ago, there was a farmer at Skaftafell named Bjarni, who was an excellent craftsman. A troll-wife lived in a cave above the Skaftafell Woods. She was friendly towards Bjarni; she guarded his sheep in the mountains and his driftwood on the shore. One winter, she said to Bjarni that a ship had run aground on the shore. All the men aboard were dead but one. The only survivor was a fearsome savage who would destroy all the south of Iceland unless he were slain. Then she took up an axe and went with Bjarni to the shore, where she did battle with the savage and slew him. This troll-wife lived for many human lifetimes and was amicably disposed towards Bjarni's descendants. Her cave is said to exist today, with a window in the middle of the roof-ridge. The troll-wife's bed is reputed to be cut into the rock, eight ells in length and two ells across [one ell is about 50 cm]. Bjarni is said to have built the cave door and all the door fittings, so that the troll-wife would be comfortable there.

Einar was a renowned man who lived at Skaftafell

in Öræfi. He is said to have known a certain troll-wife. Once, when Einar was travelling, he suddenly found himself in thick fog. He suspected that the fog was not entirely natural, but made to lead him astray. So he took an axe that he had brought with him and threw it away. The fog immediately lifted and Einar continued his journey, reaching home safe and sound. Just after this, one of his horses collapsed. He found the axe, covered with blood, on a sill outside his farmhouse.

The following year, Einar was travelling and had to cross the Skeiðará river. Before he set off to ford the river, he saw a very large woman coming towards him. When they met she asked him for the loan of his horse to cross the river. Einar was reluctant; he said he was afraid she would over-strain the horse as she did last year. The troll-wife said that she had good reason for doing so, as Einar had played a prank on her. She said that when he threw his axe away it had struck her between the breasts and she showed him the scar it had left. Einar saw that she was telling the truth and he permitted her to ride a horse he was leading. They set off across the river and crossed safely.

It is said that the troll-wife teased Einar and that he said he wished to seek her out to be revenged. He went home and made a copper gun, which still exists at Skaftafell. A little later he went to find her. The troll-wife then made her peace with him and promised to do as he wished. Einar's only demand was that she ensure against anyone stealing timber from his woods beyond the Morsá river.

SNORRI THE FUGITIVE

Þórsmörk is an upland valley that is a favourite with tourists; it boasts mountains and valleys, wildflowers and birch woods, glacial rivers and crystal-clear streams, grassland and barren sands. Majestic glaciers rise up on three sides of this mountain vastness. But natural beauty is not the only attraction for visitors to Þórsmörk: for those on the folklore trail, there is also a cave of special interest, named Snorraríki, in Húsadalur.

To reach Þórsmörk, one has to ford Krossá, a dangerous and fast-flowing river that should only be crossed with the greatest care. This route leads to Langidalur. From there, many visitors take a walk over to Húsadalur (Houses' Valley), which was once inhabited. In the Saga Age, this was the home of Björn Kaðalsson the White, who plays a part in Njál's Saga. From the head of Langidalur, the path leads up on to a ridge, then down into Húsadalur. High on the slope is a basalt cliff and high up in this cliff is a cave known as Snorraríki (Snorri's Dominion):

here was once a man named Snorri, who was probably both young and strong, for he proved most resource-ful. He had stolen something or committed some other offence, so that he found himself on the wrong side of the law. At that time the criminal code was both harsh and merciless, so Snorri decided to avoid the royal officials and ran away. A posse was raised to follow him and capture him, but the men soon found that Snorri was quick on his feet and evaded them all. He fled into the mountains, to Þórsmörk. There, Snorri was overtaken by the searchers and they finally succeeded in cornering him, so it appeared that he had no way out. But when they tried to capture this fleet-footed man, he climbed up into a cave at the top of Húsadalur. The search party soon found out where he was and decided to surround the cave and starve Snorri into submission. They could not reach him there, for the cave is so high up in the rock that one man can easily defend himself, though besieged by many. And so the search party decided to wait at the foot of the cliff until Snorri grew so hungry that he would give himself up.

But things did not go as they had foreseen. They waited there, day after day and night after night, and Snorri the fugitive showed no signs of surrendering. This had gone on for a long time and they thought that Snorri would soon succumb to starvation, when the fugitive suddenly appeared at the mouth of the cave. But he was not there to give himself up; instead, he threw a good, fat leg of lamb down to the exhausted men below and said he hoped they enjoyed it. The men were taken aback and said that there was no point in trying to starve Snorri into submission; he had so much food that he was sharing it with them! After some consultation, they decided to abandon the siege and return home.

What they did not know was that the leg of lamb Snorri had flung down to them was the only food left in the cave. He did this as a last resort and it had the desired result. When the posse had gone, Snorri climbed down from the cave and made his escape. No more is known of Snorri but such a resourceful man must surely have been able to take care of himself. After this the cave was known as Snorraríki (Snorri's Dominion), in honour of the resourceful and fleet-footed fugitive.

Today, steps have been cut into the rock, so almost anyone can climb up to Snorri's Dominion – provided he or she is wearing good walking shoes and has a head for heights. Many visitors to Þórsmörk have carved their name, initials or the date in the rock below the cave, and perhaps the initials of Snorri himself are somewhere among them. Who knows?

THE WOMAN AND THE SEALSKIN

*Mýrdalur is the region between Jökulsá on Sólheima-
sandur in the west and the Mýrdalssandur desert
in the east. This is Iceland's southernmost region, a
fertile and well-vegetated area in the shelter of the
Mýrdalsjökull glacier.*

*The landscape of Mýrdalur is picturesque, with
splendid mountains and Dyrhólaey and Reynisfjall
on the seaward side. South of Reynisfjall the Reynis-
drangar rock pillars rise up out of the sea, the highest reaching 66 m. These pillars came into existence
when two night trolls went to tow a three-masted vessel ashore. They took longer than they expected and
were caught in the rays of the rising sun, and so they
and their ship were turned to stone.*

Seals are often seen swimming offshore at Mýrdalur. According to folklore, seals came into existence when the waters of the Red Sea were parted for the children of Israel so that they could pass safely over to the other side; when Pharaoh's warriors followed them, the sea closed over them and they were turned into seals. God mercifully allows them to come ashore once a year, shed their sealskin and make merry in human form until morning. The folk tale of the woman and the sealskin from Mýrdalur suggests that such things really happened:

nce upon a time, a man in Mýrdalur was walking by the cliffs along the shore in the early morning, before anybody else was awake. He came to the mouth of a cave and inside the cave he could hear merriment and dancing, while outside lay many seal-skins. He picked one up, took it home, and locked it up in a chest. Later that day the man passed by the same place. A pretty young woman sat outside the cave, stark naked and weeping bitterly. She was the seal whose skin the man had taken that morning. He gave her clothes, comforted her and took her home. She was submissive to the man, but was reserved with others and often sat looking out to sea.

After a while they were married. They were happy together and had seven children. The farmer always kept the sealskin locked in the chest and carried the key with him wherever he went.

Many years later, the farmer went to church at Christmas with the household, while the woman stayed home, saying she was unwell. On this occasion, the farmer had left his key in his everyday clothes, when he put on his best suit. But when he returned home the chest was open, the sealskin gone and the woman, too. She had found the key, opened the chest out of curiosity and discovered her sealskin. Then she could not resist the temptation: she bade her children farewell, donned her sealskin and plunged into the sea. Before she went, she is supposed to have said:

Oh, woe is me,
I have seven children on land
and seven in the sea.

The man deeply regretted the loss of his wife, but there was nothing he could do. When he rowed out to fish after that, a seal often swam around his boat and it seemed to have tears in its eyes. After that, he always had good catches and many valuable things were washed ashore on his land. And often, when their children walked along the shore, a seal was seen swimming just offshore, keeping pace with them. Not only that, but the seal often tossed up to them many-coloured fishes and pretty shells. But their mother never came ashore again.

GOLD UNDER SKÓGAFOSS

A little farther west of Skógar is Skógafoss, one of Iceland's most beautiful and impressive waterfalls. The first settler at Skógar was named Þrasi Þórólfsson. He was said to be a great warrior, well informed and with supernatural skills. Þrasi had a dispute with Loðmundur the Aged, who had settled at Sólheimar east of the Jökulsá river. Both men had magical powers and their dispute grew ever more rancorous. One after the other, they diverted the Jökulsá river over each other's land, creating the wastelands of Sólheimasandur and Skógasandur. Eventually, they saw that neither could win the feud, so they met halfway and agreed that the river should flow the shortest route to the sea. Þrasi made his home just east of Skógafoss: probably he was impressed by the 60 m cascade, since in his old age he took a great chest full of gold and treasure, and threw it under the waterfall. The tale goes as follows:

rasi of Skógar was a man of great wealth. When he was old and felt that death was approaching, he decided that he did not want his wealth to be dispersed after his day. So he took a chest full of money and valuable goods, and sank it in the deep pool beneath the Skógafoss waterfall. There the chest has lain for century after century; for a long time, the end of the chest could be seen under the waterfall. Over the ages, many people have tried to lift the chest out but without success. Once it was a near thing, for some brave men managed to get a rope through a ring on the end of the chest. They started hauling the chest up and all went well at first. But then the ring suddenly came off its fastenings and the chest vanished into the depths. All they had left was the ring, which they took back to Skógar.

Skógar used to have a church and the idea arose of fitting the remarkable ring to the church door. But in 1890, the Skógar church was deconsecrated and demolished. The ring from the door found its way to Eyvindarhólar and was fitted to the church door there. In 1960, a new church was built at Eyvindar- hólar and the old one demolished. The ring was not used for the new door and so it went to the Skógar Folk Museum, where it is on display, one of the treas- ures of the museum's collection.

It is probably not worth diving down under Skóga- foss in search of Þrasi's treasure-chest, since this is, after all, a folk tale. But there may be a grain of truth in the tale, as witness this old verse that has been passed down from generation to generation:

> *Richly stacked is Þrasi's chest*
> *under Skógar's waters cold.*
> *Whosoever goes there first*
> *will find wealth untold.*

GILITRUTT AND
THE LAZY WIFE

Stóri-Dalur in Eyjafjallasveit was once an important manor; in the late 10th century, it was the home of Runólfur Úlfsson, the leader of the pagan faction at the Althing (parliament) of AD 1000. The antagonism between pagan and Christian threatened the very existence of the young Icelandic state, and a decision was made at parliament, to adopt Christianity. On his return home that summer, Runólfur took all his pagan idols and carried them up on to the glacier, where he placed them in a cave in a rock which projects up out of the ice-cap. This has since been called Goðasteinn (Gods' Rock).

In the east of the Eyjafjöll district is Rauðafell, where Hrafn the Foolish settled during the Age of Settlement; he was an ancestor of Sæmundur the Wise, who acquired semi-legendary status in folklore. One of Iceland's favourite folk tales recounts events reputed to have taken place on the farm of Rauðafell: this is the story of Gilitrutt. Some say she was a troll-wife, while others believe she was an elf woman; above the farmhouse at Rauðafell is a hillock that is supposed to have been Gilitrutt's home, known as Álfhóll (Elf Hill).

nce upon a time, a hardworking farmer lived in the east below the Eyjafjöll mountains. He had recently married a young woman who was lazy and indolent, and did little work about the farm. The farmer was discontented with this, but could do nothing about it. In the autumn, he brought her a great quantity of wool and asked her to weave it into cloth. She was reluctant and as the winter passed she did not touch the wool.

One day a woman of large build came to the farmer's wife and asked her for some favour. The farmer's wife asked her whether she would do something for her in return. The woman asked what that might be and the farmer's wife replied that it was to weave wool into cloth. The woman agreed and the farmer's wife handed her a big sack of wool. The woman slung the sack on to her back and said that she would bring the cloth back on the first day of summer. "What shall I pay you?" asked the farmer's wife. "Nothing much," said the woman. "Tell me what my name is at the third guess and we will be quits." The farmer's wife agreed to these terms and the woman went off with the wool. The winter passed and the farmer often asked where the wool was. His wife replied that it was none of his business and that he would have his woollen cloth on the first day of summer. He was not impressed. Time passed.

As the end of winter approached, the farmer's wife began to think about the woman's name; she could see no way of finding it out and grew melancholy over this. The farmer noticed that she was unhappy, came to her and asked what was wrong. Then she told him the whole story. The farmer was frightened and said that the woman was probably a troll-wife, who would take her away.

Some time later, the farmer was walking below the mountain slope, when he came to a stony hillock. He was deep in thought and feeling unhappy, when he heard a knocking sound inside the hillock and went closer. Finally, he found a gap in the rock and saw a large woman sitting inside, energetically weaving at a loom she held between her legs as she chanted:

> *Hi, ho, hi, ho,*
> *the farmer's wife doesn't know my name.*
> *Gilitrutt's my name, Gilitrutt's my name.*
> *Hi, ho, hi, ho.*

The farmer was cheered by this; he was sure this must be the woman who had visited his wife last autumn. He went home in a good mood and made a note of the name Gilitrutt. But he did not tell his wife what he had seen and heard. Time passed and finally, the last day of winter came around. By now the farmer's wife was so distraught that she could not get out of bed. Her husband came to her and asked if she knew the name of her helper. She said she did not and that this would be the end of her. Then the farmer comforted her, told her all that had happened, and gave her the piece of paper with the name on it. She took the paper, trembling with terror, for she feared the name might be wrong. She asked her husband to stay with her when the woman arrived, but the farmer refused; he said that she alone had made the pact about the wool, so she alone must pay the fee.

On the morning of the first day of summer, the woman lay alone in her bed; there was no one else in the house. Then she heard a great din and heavy footsteps. The large woman entered, looking far from friendly. She flung down a great roll of woollen cloth and asked: "So what's my name? What's my name?" The farmer's wife was terrified almost to death, but stammered the name "Ása." "Guess again, guess again, farmer's wife," said the woman. "Signý." "One more guess, one more guess, farmer's wife," said the woman. Then the farmer's wife plucked up courage and asked: "I don't suppose your name is Gilitrutt?" The woman was so startled that she fell down flat on the floor with a great crash. Then she jumped to her feet, rushed out and was never seen again. The farmer's wife was delighted at her escape from the creature and she changed her ways completely. She became a hardworking and conscientious farmwife, and she always wove her own wool after that.

GISSUR OF BOTNAR AND THE TROLL-WIFE

Mt. Hekla, Iceland's most beautiful and best-known volcano, rises up from the lowlands north of Rangárvellir and dominates the landscape all around. Hekla is believed to have been formed about 7,000 years ago, when the first fissure eruption occurred on the site, and its splendid mass has been built up gradually during at least 100 eruptions. In the 1,100 years since Iceland was settled, Hekla erupted an average of twice each century, until the 20th century, when it erupted six times. In the past, eruptions of Mt. Hekla were believed to presage important events, such as wars or the deaths of kings and emperors. Although such beliefs are rare today, it is interesting to note that the 1991 eruption started on 17 January, the same day as the Gulf War began and King Olaf V of Norway died.

The innermost farm on Rangárvellir is Næfurholt, which lies close to the volcano. Nearby is a picturesque, steep-sloped hill named Bjólfell. North of Næfurholt, far above the inhabited areas, is a great gorge named Tröllkonugil (Troll-wife's Gorge). West of the Þjórsá river, farther inland than Bjólfell, is a table mountain named Búrfell. This is the territory of the troll-wife of Búrfell:

Once upon a time there were two troll-wives: one lived in Mt. Búrfell and the other in Mt. Bjólfell. They were sisters and close friends. The troll-wife of Búrfell often visited her sister, travelling east across the Þjórsá and Rangá rivers to Bjólfell, and her sister probably visited her, too. Búrfell is a very rocky mountain with steep cliffs. To the east, below the middle of the hill, there are two rocks, not very high, one on either side of the Þjórsá river. Two more rocks, about the same height, stand up out of the river between them, so the river cascades down in three branches. The troll-wife of Búrfell is said to have placed these stepping-stones in the river so that she could cross it in three jumps without wetting her feet. The rocks are called Tröllkonuhlaup (Troll-wife's Leap).

Kjallakatungur is the name of an area of sand dunes and vegetation between the Þjórsá and Rangá rivers. In former times, those who travelled north to the upland pastures passed through this area.

In Landsveit there is a farm named Botnar or Lækjarbotnar. The farmer living there when this story took place was named Gissur. One day, he went in to the uplands to go fishing, taking a packhorse along. When he felt he had caught as many fish as the horse could carry, he set off homewards. Nothing is known of his journey until he reached Kjallakatungur opposite Tröllkonuhlaup, where he heard a voice thundering out of Búrfell:

"Sister, lend me a cooking pot."

"What do you want it for?" was asked from Bjólfell.

"To cook a man in it," resounded from Búrfell.

"What's his name?" was asked from Bjólfell.

"Gissur of Botnar, Gissur of Lækjarbotnar", was heard from Búrfell.

At that moment, Farmer Gissur looked up at Búrfell and saw a troll-wife come clattering down the slope, heading straight for Tröllkonuhlaup. He was convinced that she meant to put her words into action and that he must try to escape. He released the packhorse and whipped the one he was riding, a fine, light-footed mount. He rode as fast as he could, without looking back, but he could hear the troll-wife panting after him and concluded that she was catching up.

Gissur rode down through Land, with the troll-wife hard on his heels. Then he was fortunate that the people of Klofi saw him and the troll-wife, and rang all the church bells at Klofi just as Gissur reached the homefield. The troll-wife, having failed to catch Gissur, flung her axe after him; as he reached the farmhouse, his horse dropped down dead with the axe blade buried in its loins. Gissur gave sincere thanks to God for his escape from peril.

As for the troll-wife, she was so taken aback by the ringing of the bells that she went mad and ran away as fast as she could. She was seen from various farms in Land. She ran much farther than her home, heading eastwards towards Tröllkonugil; she was found there, dead of exertion, a few days later and the gully has been known since then as Tröllkonugil (Troll-wife's Gorge). Her sister of Bjólfell is not known to have threatened her neighbours and little is told of her after the demise of her sister. Some say that she moved to Tröllkonugil, not wishing to live so close to humans any more.

THE DANCE AT HRUNI

The village Flúðir has grown up around an area of hot springs. Close to the village is Hruni, which was once an important manor. From the late 12th century and into the 13th, Þorvaldur Gissurarson, a magnate of the Haukadalur clan, was pastor at Hruni. In 1224, he was one of those who founded a monastery on the island of Viðey, off the coast of Reykjavík. His son (priests were not required to be celibate in those days) was Gissur Þorvaldsson, who played an important role in Icelandic affairs in the 13th century and is the only earl in Icelandic history.

Many remarkable pastors have served the parish of Hruni over the centuries, including Jón Héðinsson. At the height of the Reformation in 1539, when foreign bishops were attempting to force the new Lutheran order upon the Icelandic church, the Rev. Jón raised a posse to kill the Danish governor's henchman, Didrik von Minden, who had been pillaging monasteries and harassing monks.

Another pastor who served at Hruni is not known by name, though he is the subject of a well-known folk tale. Long ago, the church at Hruni stood on a hilltop above the farmhouse. The folk tale tells of how the church site came to be moved down to the lowlands near the farm:

There was once a pastor at Hruni who loved revels and entertainments. It was the custom of this pastor, when people came to church to attend Mass on Christmas Night, not to have any religious service during the early part of the night, as was usual, but instead to hold an entertainment for the parishioners, with dancing, drinking, games and other unseemly behaviour far into the night. The pastor's mother, whose name was Una, was with him at Hruni. She strongly disapproved of her son's behaviour and she often expressed her dissatisfaction to him. But he paid no attention and continued in the same way for many years.

One Christmas Night, the pastor remained longer at this dance in the church than was usual for him. His mother, who had the second sight and prophetic powers, went over to the church and asked her son to leave the dance and go to Mass. He protested that there was plenty of time and said: "One more turn, Mother, one more turn", and the dance went on. Una walked out of the church and into the farmhouse, but she was not happy and she returned a second and a third time to ask her son to think of God and give up the dance, before things went awry. He replied as before: "One more turn, Mother, one more turn," and the dance went on. But when Una walked down the aisle for the third time, she heard the following:

Hruni rings out in cheer,
the crowds draw near;
the dance will fill the air
remembered forever;
Una still is there
and Una still is there.

When Una came out of the church, she saw a man standing outside. She did not know him, but did not like the look of him. She was sure that this man had spoken the verse. She was taken aback and saw that things had indeed gone awry, for it was the Devil himself.

She took her son's horse and rode as fast as she could to the pastor of the next parish. She told him the whole story and asked him to come and rescue her son, if possible, from the danger he was in. The pastor agreed at once, gathered together a large group from the congregation of his church and returned to Hruni with Una. But they were too late. When they arrived at Hruni, the church, the pastor and all his flock had vanished down into the bowels of the earth, and only howls and screams could be heard.

A new church was built below the hill after this and since then all the churches of Hruni have stood in the new location. But up on the hill, there are still traces of a building that once stood there. The story says that after these terrifying events, there was never again dancing at Hruni on Christmas Night.

THE MERMAN LAUGHED

Vogar is a thriving community on Faxaflói bay, with about 1,100 inhabitants. This was once the manor of Stóru-Vogar, with many small farms around it where people made their living by a combination of animal husbandry and fishing. In the late 19th century, Vogar began to grow into a village, especially after it became a licensed trading port in 1893. South of Vogar is Vogastapi, with steep cliffs down to the sea. Below it were rich fishing grounds in former times, known as Gullkista (Treasure Chest). Ghosts have long been reputed to haunt Vogastapi, and in past centuries, many people lost their way there and fell to their deaths from the cliffs or died of exposure. Even today, rumours are heard of hauntings; motorists on the main road have been known to see a man walking with his head under his arm. The Stapi Ghost sometimes even joins people in their cars, if they are travelling alone in dark conditions.

The people of the district have long made their living from the sea and they have a reputation for being determined fishermen, who were not easily discouraged. Once the farmer of Vogar caught a merman on his hook, as the folk tale tells:

In the Suðurnes region, there is a hamlet named Vogar, or Kvíguvogar as it is called in the Book of Settlements. Once a farmer lived there who was a keen fisherman, for the place has some of the best fishing in all south Iceland. One day, the farmer rowed out as usual and nothing is told of the fish he caught. But he hooked something heavy and when he had pulled it up by the boat, he saw that it was of human shape and hauled it aboard. The farmer discovered that the man was alive and he asked him where he was from. The man said he was a merman from the bottom of the sea. He said he had been caught by the farmer's hook when he was fixing his mother's kitchen chimney. He asked the farmer to let him go down again, but the farmer said that was not possible and that the merman would have to stay with him. After that the merman would not speak to him.

A short while later the farmer went ashore, taking the merman with him. When he had beached his vessel, his dog came down to him and jumped up to greet him. The farmer was angry and struck the dog a blow. Then the merman laughed for the first time. The farmer went on up the homefield and tripped over a tussock and cursed it. Then the merman laughed a second time. The farmer went on to the farmhouse. His wife came out and greeted him affectionately and he responded warmly to her welcome. Then the merman laughed a third time.

The farmer said to the merman: "You have laughed three times and I am curious to know why you laughed." "I won't tell you," said the merman, "unless you take me back to the place where you caught me." The farmer agreed. Then the merman said: "I laughed for the first time when you struck your dog, for he came to greet you with affection. I laughed again when you tripped over the tussock and cursed it, for it is full of gold. And I laughed for the third time when you happily received the cant of your wife, for she deceives you and is unfaithful. Now you must fulfil your promise to me and return me to the fishing grounds where you caught me."

The farmer said: "Two of the things you said – the affection of my dog and the faithfulness of my wife – cannot be tested at present, but I shall test the truth of what you say about gold being hidden in the tussock. If this is so, it is more likely that the other things are true too, and I shall fulfil my promise."

Then the farmer went and dug up the tussock. He found a hoard of money there, as the merman had said. Then he launched his vessel and returned the merman to the same fishing grounds where he had caught him. But before the farmer released him, the merman said: "You have acted well, farmer, in returning me to my mother, and I shall repay you, if you know how to make use of what you receive. Farewell, farmer." Then the farmer let him down into the depths and no more is said of the merman. But the merman's laughter is commemorated by a rhyme:

> *I remember his laughter,*
> *the merman's, so loud;*
> *sweet his treasure after*
> *landwards he rowed;*
> *he kissed the fair maid*
> *though false she was found,*
> *but the great hero flayed*
> *his poor blameless hound.*

Shortly after this, the farmer was told that seven cows, sea-grey in colour, were at the edge of the homefield by the sea. He responded quickly, grabbing a staff as he went. He went to where the cows were; they were restless and uneasy. He noticed that each cow had a bladder over her mouth, and he realised that he would lose the cows unless he could burst the bladders. He struck at the face of one cow and managed to catch her but all the others escaped into the sea. Now the farmer concluded that the merman had sent him the cows in thanks for releasing him. The cow he caught proved to be the most excellent beast known in Iceland. Cattle descended from her were dispersed all over Iceland, all grey in colour, and known as the "sea-cow breed". The farmer became a wealthy man, and changed the name of Vogar (Bays) to Kvíguvogar (Heifer Bays), after the cows that had come ashore there.

Jón R. Hjálmarsson (1922–2018) was a historian and educator and served as a school principal and later as regional administrator of education in south Iceland for many years. He was well known as a broadcaster, tour guide and author of several popular books on history and folktales.

25 Icelandic folk and fairy tales
© Jón R. Hjálmarsson 2019
English translation © Anna Yates 2019

Layout and cover design: Halla Sigga / Forlagið
Illustrations: Halla Sigga / Forlagið
Main font: Grad 10/14 pt
Printing: Almarose, Slovenia

1st edition 2019
Reprinted 2021, 2022, 2023

Published in Reykjavík, a UNESCO City of Literature

Forlagið · Reykjavík · 2023

ISBN 978-9979-53-705-2

www.forlagid.is